HOLE-IN-ONE ADVERBS

By Doris Fisher and D. L. Gibbs
Cover illustrated by Scott Angle
Interior illustrated by Jeff Chandler
Curriculum consultant: Candia Bowles, M.Ed., M.S.

Gareth Stevens
Publishing

Please visit our web site at **www.garethstevens.com**.
For a free color catalog describing Gareth Stevens Publishing's list of high-quality books, call 1-800-542-2595 (USA) or 1-800-387-3178 (Canada). Gareth Stevens Publishing's fax: 1-877-542-2596

Library of Congress Cataloging-in-Publication Data

Fisher, Doris.
    Grammar all-stars / Doris Fisher and D. L. Gibbs.
      p. cm.
    ISBN-10: 0-8368-8902-9   ISBN-13: 978-0-8368-8902-4 (lib. bdg.)
    ISBN-10: 0-8368-8909-6   ISBN-13: 978-0-8368-8909-3 (pbk.)
    1. English language—Grammar—Juvenile literature. 2. English language—Parts of speech—Juvenile literature. 3. Sports—Juvenile literature. I. Gibbs, D.L. II. Title.
    PE1112.F538   2008
    428.2—dc22   2007033840

This edition first published in 2008 by
Gareth Stevens Publishing
A Weekly Reader® Company
1 Reader's Digest Road
Pleasantville, NY 10570-7000 USA

Copyright © 2008 by Gareth Stevens, Inc.

Senior Managing Editor: Lisa M. Guidone
Senior Editor: Barbara Bakowski
Creative Director: Lisa Donovan
Senior Designer: Keith Plechaty

Printed in the United States of America

1 2 3 4 5 6 7 8 9 10 09 08 07

CONTENTS

Look for the **boldface** words on each page.
Then read the **HOLE-IN-ONE HINT** that follows.

CHAPTER 1

ON THE COURSE

What Are Adverbs?

"Greetings from Lost Ball Golf Course. I'm Buzz Star for P-L-A-Y TV, reporting **live** at the final round of the King of Swing Classic. The golfer to beat is Ace Puttman. Ace **recently** won the Back Nine Invitational. But do **not** overlook Birdie Bunker and Chip Away. One of these three golfers will **surely** capture the King of Swing trophy."

Buzz smiles. "I have another golf champion **here** with me **today**," he says. "Alex Todd is a master at miniature golf. He is **also** my kid reporter for the day. Tell us about your mini-golf award, Alex."

"I had the best score at Putt-Putt Paradise in June," says Alex. "**Now** I get to play **free**. I **also** get lessons from a golf pro."

"Are you **really** good, Alex?" asks Buzz. "Or are you **just** lucky?"

"I play **well**," says Alex. "Miniature golf is my favorite sport. When I **first** started, I played bad." He groans. "No, wait. I mean, **badly**."

"*Bad . . . badly . . .* Everyone makes mistakes **sometimes**," says Buzz.

"I know," says Alex, "but my dad is an English teacher. He **always** tells me to watch my adverbs."

"Does your dad tell you to watch your golf swing, **too**?" asks Buzz.

Alex laughs **softly**. "Yes, he **often** gives me pointers," says Alex. "My dad taught me to play golf **here**, at Lost Ball Golf Course."

HOLE-IN-ONE HINT

ADVERB

An **adverb** describes a **verb**, an **adjective**, or **another adverb**. An **adverb** can tell **how**, **when**, or **where**.

How many **adverbs** can you find on pages 4 to 8?

"The crowd is waiting **patiently** for the golfers to tee off," Buzz continues. "While we pass the time, Alex, tell our viewers about the course."

"Lost Ball is a tough golf course," says Alex. "The rough is **really** rough. But the greens are **closely** mowed, so the golfers can putt **easily**."

"Folks, I see our three golfers **slowly** but **surely** making their way to the first tee," says Buzz. "I'll let my sidekick describe the action."

Alex speaks **quietly**. "Ace Puttman **carefully** places his ball on the tee. He swings **smoothly** and hits a long drive. His ball **safely** lands in the fairway."

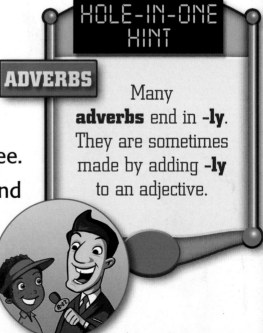

HOLE-IN-ONE HINT

ADVERBS

Many **adverbs** end in **-ly**. They are sometimes made by adding **-ly** to an adjective.

"Birdie Bunker tees off," says Buzz. "He hits the ball **far**, and it **just** lands on the green. Birdie seems **very** nervous. He has played this course **just once**."

"**Now** Chip Away pulls a driver from his bag," Alex says. "He leans **forward** and swings the club **hard**. Oh, that's a whiff! Chip swings **again**, and this time his ball lands in the rough. He is **not** happy with that shot."

"Chip will have to play **better** if he hopes to shoot par," Bud says. The announcer shakes his head as Chip's next shot heads **straight** for the lake.

"Chip's play is **no** better on the second hole," Alex comments **later**. "He teed off **first**, slicing his ball **far**. **Now** he is shouting 'Fore!' to warn the crowd. This may be a long afternoon, folks."

HOLE-IN-ONE HINT

ADVERBS

Some **adverbs** do NOT end in **-ly**.

TEE TIME

How? When? Where?

"Ladies and gentlemen, the King of Swing Classic is in full swing. Our golfers have finished nine holes of play. Some played more **skillfully** than others, and we saw a mix of birdies and bogeys. Alex talked **briefly** to some of the pros as they made their way along the course," says Buzz. "Can you **quickly** tell us what they had to say, Alex?"

"I asked each player three questions. The first question was '*How* is your golf game?' Ace Puttman said, 'I play **brilliantly**.' Birdie Bunker said, 'I play **skillfully**.' Chip Away said, 'I play **wildly**!'"

HOLE-IN-ONE HINT

ADVERB

An **adverb** can tell **how**.

"That was a good question, Alex," says Buzz. "What did you ask **next**?"

"I asked, '*When* do you practice?'" says Alex. "Ace said, 'I practice **daily**.' Birdie said, 'I practice **often**.' Chip said, 'I **never** practice!'"

"You are a mini-golf master, Alex. Do you practice **frequently**?" Buzz asks.

"I do," Alex replies. "I played two rounds **yesterday**. And I will practice at Putt-Putt Paradise **tomorrow**."

"I **always** say practice makes perfect," Buzz jokes.

HOLE-IN-ONE HINT

ADVERB

An **adverb** can tell **when**.

"When I asked, '*Where* do you practice?' Ace told me he practices **outdoors**. Birdie said, 'I practice **anywhere**.' Chip said, 'I practice **nowhere**!'"

"Hmm," says Buzz, scratching his head. "I wonder how Chip Away became one of this event's top three golfers! So far, he has stumbled **here**. On the fourth hole, his wild swings sent divots flying **everywhere**! On the seventh hole, his ball landed outside the green, in a sand trap. As Chip blasted out of the bunker, sand covered the fans standing **nearby**."

HOLE-IN-ONE HINT

ADVERB

An **adverb** can tell **where**.

"With nine holes left, Mr. Star, do you want to predict the champion?" asks Alex.

"Well, Ace Puttman leads, at four under par. That makes him the favorite to win," says Buzz. "Birdie Bunker is just two strokes off the lead. If Birdie shines on the back nine, he has a chance to grab the victory. Chip Away has trailed on every hole, so I'd say he's a long shot.

"Viewers, stay with us at P-L-A-Y TV as we bring you the exciting action live from Lost Ball Golf Course!"

CHAPTER 3

PAR "FORE!" THE COURSE

Using Adverbs

"Ladies and gentlemen," says Buzz, "our golfers have **finally** reached the eighteenth hole. I thought we'd **never** get **here**! Chip Away is playing **poorly**, trailing **behind** on every hole," Buzz continues. "His shots **seldom** land on the green. They **always** find a sand trap or a pond."

"How many balls has Chip lost in this round?" asks Alex.

"Seven, at last count," says Buzz. "Chip **rarely** lines up his shots. He **sometimes** swings **crazily**. Let's watch as Ace Puttman tees off. Take over, Alex."

HOLE-IN-ONE HINT

ADVERB

Many times, an **adverb** describes a **verb**.

"Ace looks **extremely** calm as he steps up to the tee," Alex says. "His game has been **almost** perfect. The **already** quiet crowd becomes **even** quieter. Ace pulls a **fairly** long driver from his bag. Now he takes a **truly** mighty swing and … I don't believe it! Ace Puttman missed the ball! He looks **totally** teed off, Buzz."

whiff!

"You are **surely** correct, Alex," Buzz replies. "That was a **somewhat** unusual mistake."

Alex nods. "Ace seems to have lost his cool. He takes a **badly** aimed whack at the ball. Oh, no! The ball bounces off an **extremely** tall tree and rolls a few feet behind the tee."

Ace's **very** bad luck continues. His next shot is **hardly** better than the first two.

"That was a **completely** unexpected flop by Ace," says Buzz. "He cannot be **entirely** sure of a win."

HOLE-IN-ONE HINT

ADVERB

Sometimes, an **adverb** describes an **adjective**.

"It's Birdie Bunker's turn to tee off," says Alex. "His ball **just** barely avoids a bunker before landing on the green. The crowd cheers **very** loudly, and Birdie waves **quite** happily to the fans."

"Now Chip Away steps up to the tee," Buzz says. "He swings **really** sharply, and his ball soars **incredibly** high. It clears the fairway … it's on the green and … it's a hole in one!"

ONE!

The fans roar **more** wildly. "Unless Ace and Birdie putt **extremely** well, Chip may win the King of Swing Classic," says Alex.

"Birdie Bunker steps onto the green," says Alex. "Wow, what a long putt! The fans hold their breath as the ball rolls **so** slowly toward the hole. Oh, it just lips out! Birdie sets up again and taps the ball **especially** softly. The crowd groans as the ball veers **just** wide."

HOLE-IN-ONE HINT

ADVERBS

An **adverb** can describe **other adverbs**.

"Birdie will not catch Chip Away, ladies and gentlemen!" says Buzz. "He finally sinks his putt and stomps angrily off the course. Now all eyes are on Ace Puttman as he slowly approaches the green. If Ace misses this putt, Chip will walk off with the trophy."

Alex is almost too nervous to watch. "Ace lines up his shot. But just as he swings, a nearby fan sneezes loudly. Ace turns his head sharply, taking his eye off the ball. He watches in disbelief as it rolls far beyond the hole."

"And so ends the King of Swing Golf Classic!" says Buzz. "Chip Away came from behind to ace the final hole and win the tournament. Alex, do you have any winning advice for our viewers?"

"Sure, Buzz. Always wear old socks when you play golf. You might have a hole in one."

Buzz chuckles. "Thanks for helping me today, Alex. I hope all your rounds at Putt-Putt Paradise are par for the course."

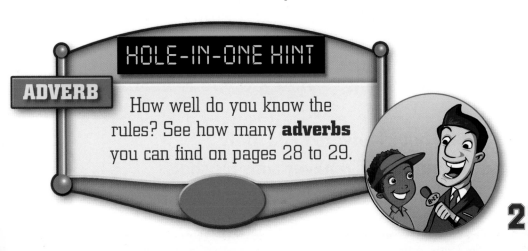

HOLE-IN-ONE HINT

ADVERB

How well do you know the rules? See how many **adverbs** you can find on pages 28 to 29.

BUZZ STAR PLAYS BY THE RULES!

An **adverb** describes a **verb**, an **adjective**, or **another adverb**.
Examples: The crowd waits **patiently**.
The rough is **really** rough.
Alex plays **very** well.

An **adverb** can tell **how**.
Example: The greens are **closely** mowed.

An **adverb** can tell **when**.
Example: Ace Puttman practices **daily**.

An **adverb** can tell **where**.
Example: His wild swings sent divots
flying **everywhere**!

Many **adverbs** end in **-ly**.
Example: Ace's ball **rarely** lands in the rough.

BUT not all **adverbs** end in **-ly**.
Example: Chip **never** aims his shots.
He swings **again**.

Alex wrote a sports article for his school newspaper.

Can you find all the adverbs in his story?

I watched a round of golf with Buzz Star yesterday. We announced the King of Swing Classic on TV station P-L-A-Y. Ace Puttman, Birdie Bunker, and Chip Away played eagerly for the tournament trophy. The fans watched silently from the sidelines.

Onlookers watch quietly at Putt-Putt Paradise Mini Golf Course, too. I play miniature golf there. I always aim carefully, and I sink most putts perfectly. The hole I like least is the one with the windmill!

At the King of Swing Classic, Ace Puttman often made terrific shots. Birdie Bunker played skillfully. Most of Chip Away's shots landed in the rough. He rarely shot par. But he made a hole in one on the eighteenth hole!

Ace and Birdie needed to putt very cautiously on the final green. Birdie putted poorly and stomped angrily off the course. Ace made a bad putt and fell behind. Some really bad luck cost him the win. A fan who was standing nearby sneezed loudly. Startled, Ace hit the ball too hard. It flew beyond the green. He looked everywhere for his lost ball but never found it.

The trophy ceremony took place afterward. A crowd waited outside for autographs. Chip gladly signed photos for his fans.

Later, Buzz and I went home. We were hungry, so my mom made a special lunch: club sand-wedges!

On a piece of paper, list all of the **adverbs** in Alex's article.

All-Star Challenge

Look at each adverb on your list. Decide whether it tells **how**, **when**, or **where**.

Turn the page to check your answers and to see how many points you scored!

ANSWER KEY

Did you find enough adverbs to score a hole in one?

0–7 adverbs: Bogey (oops!)   **16–23** adverbs: Birdie

8–15 adverbs: Par   **24–30** adverbs: HOLE IN ONE!

ADVERBS

1. yesterday	**9.** perfectly	**17.** angrily	**25.** never
2. eagerly	**10.** least	**18.** behind	**26.** afterward
3. silently	**11.** often	**19.** really	**27.** outside
4. quietly	**12.** skillfully	**20.** nearby	**28.** gladly
5. too	**13.** rarely	**21.** loudly	**29.** later
6. there	**14.** very	**22.** too	**30.** home
7. always	**15.** cautiously	**23.** hard	
8. carefully	**16.** poorly	**24.** everywhere	

All-Star Challenge

ADVERBS THAT TELL HOW		ADVERBS THAT TELL WHEN	ADVERBS THAT TELL WHERE
1. eagerly	**10.** cautiously	**18.** yesterday	**25.** there
2. silently	**11.** poorly	**19.** always	**26.** behind
3. quietly	**12.** angrily	**20.** often	**27.** nearby
4. too	**13.** really	**21.** rarely	**28.** everywhere
5. carefully	**14.** loudly	**22.** never	**29.** outside
6. perfectly	**15.** too	**23.** afterward	**30.** home
7. least	**16.** hard	**24.** later	
8. skillfully	**17.** gladly		
9. very			